Introduction

The aim of this book is to equip you with a host of ideas to help you take your reading to the next level. No longer will you have to trudge through books at a snail's pace. After reading this

3

guide, you will be prepared for the fast lane with all the speed readers who have learnt these secrets. Your reading list will shrink rapidly as you devour books at a speed you only dreamt of before.

This is the second edition of what was a shorter book, now containing more ideas on how to read faster and new advice on using multi-step strategies for greater comprehension and retention. This edition offers an altogether more complete presentation of what it means to be an effective reader.

How to Use This Book

The purpose of this book is to be as fundamental as possible. It contains only what is necessary to read faster and with more skill. Nothing has been added that is not 100 percent useful. Therefore, take notes and avoid overlooking any section. I suggest reading this book more than once to ensure that the more developed ideas and strategies make sense. However, also feel free to "dip in and out" to reaffirm anything you are unsure of.

Please note that developing your reading habits is an on-going process, and attempting to apply all of this book's techniques at once is unrealistic. Take time and be patient while working to improve your reading skills.

This book has been divided into two sections in order to make the subject easier to comprehend. The first section focuses on "direct" speed reading techniques. These approaches will alter how you interact with a text in a fundamental manner. Consequently, they will take time to adapt to and master.

The second section of the book introduces speed reading techniques that are "non-direct." These methods are based on leveraging your reading to focus on high value areas of a text. Many of these techniques will also boost comprehension and retention. Later chapters focus specifically on how to strengthen your reading in these areas.

On the next page is a Venn diagram that illustrates the nature of this book's two section divide.

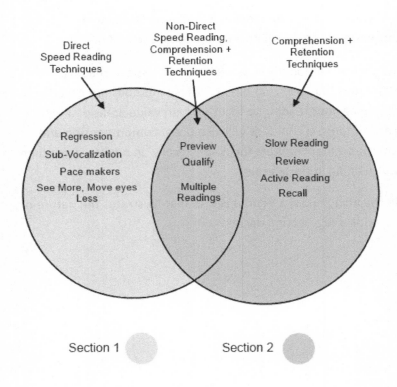

Toward the end of the book, we will explore how these techniques can be integrated into multi-step reading strategies. These strategies will allow you to meet a variety of reading goals and make you a more rounded and effective reader.

Below is a diagram that situates the first section, "direct speed reading techniques", within an example multi-step reading strategy.

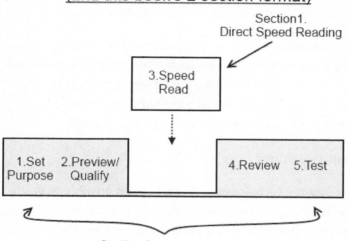

An Example Multi Step Reading Strategy (and this book's 2 section format)

Section1.
Direct Speed Reading

3.Speed Read

1.Set Purpose   2.Preview/ Qualify

4.Review   5.Test

Section 2.
Becoming an Effective Reader,
non-direct speed reading,
retention and comprehension

Don't worry if these diagrams aren't entirely understandable right now. The concepts, and how they align with one another, will become clear in time.

Introducing Speed Reading

The average reader, who has not learnt speed reading techniques, reads at a rate of roughly two hundred words per minute. There are various reasons for this, but most importantly this rate is significantly lower than it could be.

Most people assume that the rate they read at currently is the speed at which they must read. Or at least, they believe there is no way to increase their reading speed without losing all comprehension. Others assume their reading speed is a line drawn in the sand; a hard fact that cannot be altered.

This simply is not true.

By practicing the techniques in this book, it is possible to vastly increase the speed at which you read. It is possible to double and triple reading speeds to six hundred words per minute or more.

However, it is important to understand that speed reading is not going to be a like-for-like swap. The normal way of reading you learnt at school, and have used thus far, will still often be the best way to read. You cannot speed read at 600 wpm (words per minute) and have the same experience with the text when reading normally, at the rate of 200 wpm. Therefore, it is beneficial to think of speed reading as a tool most useful when reading certain texts with certain objectives.

When speed reading, a different kind of comprehension will be experienced. Often you will be able to grasp wider concepts exceptionally well but miss finer details. Short-term retention is possible with speed reading, but long-term retention can decrease dramatically. However, techniques in section two can effectively mitigate this.

It is important to align your reading techniques with both the nature of the text and your reading goals. For example, it is ridiculous to speed read poetry because you have neither the same interaction with the sounds of the words nor the time to take in the emotion of the phrases compared to normal reading. However, speed reading is of excellent help when reading a popular psychology book because the wider ideas are important, but the sounds and emotions of the text are largely irrelevant.

It should also be noted that experience with speed reading varies significantly between readers. The following factors can influence how well you progress: intelligence, ability to think in parallel, and reading experience.

Find Your Current Reading Speed

The first step to improving your reading speed is to discover your current rate. Ascertaining the exact number of words per minute you are currently reading will be very helpful as a benchmark.

With this figure in mind, you can compare reading rates as you begin to implement new techniques.

First, choose a book to read - ideally, a non-fiction book that is not too complex, either in a field you are familiar with, and/or on a topic that is fairly uncomplicated. By reading a book that fulfills these criteria, you will find a reading speed that is representative of your overall reading.

Then work through the following steps:

Find the average number of words per line. To do this, count the total number of words in the first seven lines of the book. Divide this number by seven to find the average. This will provide a sufficiently accurate average number of words-per-line for the book.

Make a mark at the first line where you are going to start reading. Using a stopwatch, time yourself reading for one minute. Read silently and at the speed you would normally. At the end of the minute, mark the line you reach.

Count the number of lines you have read. Then multiply this number by the average number of words per line (the figure from step 1).

Make a note of this number. This is your current reading speed measured in words per minute.

Perform this protocol and make a note of your score each time you master a new reading technique. Doing so will help you accurately keep track of progress.

Section One: "Direct" Speed Reading Techniques
Technique 1: Stop Backtracking

Re-reading text you have already read is a habit that can needlessly hamper your reading speed. You may not be aware that you do this, but likely you often do.

Take some time now to read a book normally. You will notice that occasionally your eyes drift back to text that you have already read. Sometimes this is to gain clarity, but other times it is for no discernable reason. Becoming aware of this bad habit is a great first step.

As a general rule, regressing and re-reading is unnecessary. If we do not fully understand what we have just read and need further clarity, we re-read consciously. However, even then re-reading a text is usually unnecessary because continuing to read will improve contextual comprehension and clarify what we were previously unsure of. Re-reading or "backtracking" is, therefore, usually a waste of time. So give your mind more credit, and work to keep your eyes from drifting backwards. Always make an effort to move forward through a text.

In order to rid yourself of the habit of backtracking, simply trace your finger under the text as you read, and make sure it is always moving forward and never back. This will make you more conscious of where you are in the text and prevent you from back-tracking.

Technique 2: See More, and Move Your Eyes Less

Fixating on every word is another barrier to higher reading speeds. It is a reading habit that we learn as children. Although it is perhaps the only way we can learn to read, fixating on every word in a passage is not needed to understand it. The time your eyes spend moving between words, although small, can be reduced, thereby increasing your overall reading speed.

To become aware of how you can see more by fixating on only one place, focus your sight in the middle of a sentence. Notice that you can read the words around the central word. Indeed, without moving your sight from the center, you may be able to read the whole sentence with your eyes resting on just this one place.

On the next page is a text that is dissected by circles. Whilst keeping your focus on the red dot, attempt to expand your field of vision so that you also see the circles around it and the words within them. You should be able to read the first five words of the paragraph by only fixating on the red dot. The text is taken from my book, *Total Mind Maps*.

Having one central topic means that analysis comes naturally with mind mapping. Analysis can be defined as "the deconstruction of an idea into its constituent parts in order to better understand it".

If you are struggling to see the words around the word "central", relax your eyes, and make them feel slightly lazy. Weaken your gaze, and soon you will be able to see more than you did before.

A useful extension of this technique is to draw two lines down the page to dissect it into thirds. Then, move your focus ONLY between these two lines. On the next page is a text to practice this technique with. Try reading it by only stopping your eyes twice for each line of the text, whenever the line of text is intersected by a blue line.

Having one central topic means that analysis comes naturally with mind mapping. Analysis can be defined as: "the deconstruction of an idea into its constituent parts in order to better understand it".

To analyze a topic, first write it at the center of the mind map. Then decide on the main sub topics to break it into. This may take multiple iterations, so improve drafts each time until you discover the most logical disassembly. Then divide topics repeatedly until you have completely deconstructed the subject.

Using mind maps in this way allows a really deep analysis to be easily created and clearly presented. There are many times when deconstructing a topic can be helpful to improve understanding; using mind maps to do this is both intuitive and thorough.

Now try this technique with the book you have been practicing with. Draw lines, lightly in pencil if the book isn't your own, down the page at intervals. Space these lines so that there are roughly three to five words on each side of the lines, just like in the picture above. Read by moving your focus between the blue lines so that your eyes zigzag down the page.

The pencil lines are helpful to start with, but once you have practiced this technique you will grow accustomed to guessing where best to fixate your eyes. Don't worry; you won't have to draw lines onto everything you read in future!

SIDE NOTE

These first two techniques (reducing eye fixations and ceasing to backtrack) are a great entry to learning to speed read. This is because, essentially, they remove blocks rather than push for speed. Consequently, these two techniques don't require a lot of practice to reach good comprehension.

Technique 3: Grouping

The reader understands words one at a time when reading normally. With the previous chapter's techniques, despite reading with fewer eye fixations, you still understand words one at a time. However, it is possible to look at a phrase and understand it without looking at each word individually. Reading like this, in groups of words, is faster because you can understand a group of words just as well as you do single words.

To clarify, with the previous technique you learnt how to fixate less often. You looked at the center of five words, and read them consecutively (i.e., whilst focusing on Word 3, you read consecutively: Word 1, Word 2, Word 3, Word 4, Word 5).

With this new "grouping" technique you will read all five words at once whilst still holding your focus on "Word 3". You will learn to read them in one snapshot of information (i.e., you read: Words 1-5 all at once whilst focusing on Word 3).

To practice this, again draw lines down the page and dissect it into thirds. Then focus only on the points where the drawn lines dissect the text. But now, instead of reading each word, try and take in the group of words altogether so that you see two groups of words for each line of text. Force yourself to continue even if comprehension is bad. It will return. And again, work to relax your eyes and keep going. Slowly your comprehension will return, and things will make sense as your mind adjusts to reading in phrases.

When practicing, it is best to dissect the page in the same proportions as you did with "Technique 2: See More, Move Your Eyes Less," with three to five words on each side of the dividing pencil lines. Attaining comprehension of word groups this size should be achievable with less than four hours of practice.

Grouping words together to understand them all at once, is a technique that builds excellently on the previous "See More, and Move Your Eyes Less" technique. However, this is a more difficult technique to learn, and more time may be needed to learn this technique than the previous techniques. Your mind will need time to adjust, as understanding entire phrases at a time is a new skill. Set a timer, and keep moving your eyes between the dissecting lines. Comprehension will return in time, and you will be reading a lot more quickly.

This technique is best utilized when attempting to take in wider concepts of a text and when you don't need to understand the details, and also when multiple passes of the text are planned to sharpen comprehension (this will be explained in detail later).

Technique 4: Reducing Subvocalization

Reducing subvocalization will further increase your reading speed. It will allow you to learn visually instead of aurally, and will ensure that you are no longer constrained to read only as fast as you can speak.

When we learn to read as children, we read aloud. Reading aloud is a form of aural learning because we rely on understanding words via their sound. When we grow up, reading aloud progresses to "silent reading." However, this is still learning in an aural manner. The only difference is that we are saying each word to ourselves rather than verbalizing it aloud.

It is necessary to "sound out" each word when learning to read. How else would a teacher know that a child understands the combination of letters correctly? However, once we have developed adequate reading skills and recognize every word, it isn't necessary to read and learn in this way. Now we can recognize and understand words just by looking at them. At this point, reading becomes visual learning rather than aural learning and speed is greatly increased.

To become conscious of how you currently sub-vocalize words, look at a word and notice that you cannot help but "say" it to yourself in your mind.

By sub-vocalizing words and reading aurally, we limit how fast we read to the rate at which we speak. As it is possible to understand words by just looking at them, we can switch to learning visually in order to read faster. Take the time now to read a longer passage. Notice how you can understand words without saying each to yourself.

It simply isn't necessary to sound out every word to understand the majority of sentences. However, on occasion, subvocalization will be necessary, e.g., when reading new words, technical words, difficult words, and unexpected words. Most of the time, however, removing subvocalization is an efficient way to increase reading speed.

There are three levels that subvocalization can take on. Within the first level, the reader moves their lips and mouths each word they read. Children who have just begun to read silently do this. Adults who are not regular readers may also find themselves within this level.

If you move your lips whilst reading, the following techniques will discourage you from this habit:

Clench a wooden spoon, or similar object, between your teeth.

Hold water in your mouth.

Put your hand over your mouth. This will subconsciously remind you not to speak.

Lightly hold your tongue between your teeth.

The second level of subvocalization occurs when the reader still vocalizes the sounds, but in their larynx (throat). At this stage, muscles in the reader's throat move instead of their lips.

The third level of subvocalization is when the reader says the words in their mind. This is the most common form of subvocalization.

Levels two and three can be overcome by saying something else silently in your head instead of the words you are reading. For example, as you read, try to sub-vocalize, "One, two, three, four," or the letters, "A, B, C, D," each time that your eyes fixate on a new place.

Time yourself reading now, for one minute, whilst saying the letters, "A, B, C, D" repeatedly in your head. Each time your eyes fixate on a new place, say the letter/number in your mind instead of the word. Notice how it becomes easier and faster to read without saying every word to yourself. Your comprehension will be poorer than usual, but you should notice that much of the text still makes sense. With practice, comprehension will improve to a higher level.

Subvocalization limits your reading speed to the speed you can talk. The mind is capable of receiving information at a faster rate than the speed of speech, and it is capable of learning visually rather than aurally. By sub-vocalizing sounds other than the words on the page, you will cut down your reliance on sounding every word out and be able to read much faster.

It is, however, not desirable to remove subvocalization completely. Even after drilling subvocalization of other sounds, you may still find yourself sub-vocalizing certain key words or phrases without control. This is often necessary, and indeed encouraged, as the small boost subvocalization provides for comprehension is necessary for high value and/or difficult sections of text. Consider yourself successful if you get to the point where you only sub-vocalize a handful of words on each page.

Technique 5: Bringing It All Together and Forcing Speed with Pace Makers

The best way to circumvent old reading habits is to use a physical item as a "pace maker" for your eyes as they move across the page.

The protocol here is straightforward. Take a pencil or similar object, and holding it flat against the page, move it along just below the words at the speed you want to read. Read quickly, at a faster pace than you typically do, and wait for your mind to become accustomed to this speed. It will take time for comprehension to return.

One second per line of text is a verifiable and easily implemented time space for practicing, so begin here. To practice reading like this, get a clock that ticks loudly. Then, when reading, move your pace maker in time with each "tick." Alternatively, count in your head, "one Mississippi, two Mississippi," so that you work through the text at the rate of one second per line. The 2nd method, counting in your head, will also remove sub vocalizing, further boosting your reading speed. The 2nd method is also more practical as you don't need a ticking clock. Once you have mastered reading at the rate of second per line, work to increase the rate you read to two lines per second.

Speed reading like this forces your mind and eyes to read at the rate you want. Consequently, you must be patient in waiting for comprehension to return. It might take minutes reading at this rate or it might take hours, but in time you will adapt.

You can combine using a pace maker with the "grouping" technique to gain even more speed. To do this, draw lines to dissect the page or simply use your judgment as you read and guess what roughly constitutes a third of the text. Then swing the pencil, like a pendulum, between the dissecting lines, and take in a group of words at each point. Count seconds in your head to make sure you continue at a quick rate. This can be one second per line or two lines per second. Reading in this way utilizes all of the speed reading techniques you have learnt so far.

SIDE NOTE

It is a good idea to use a pace maker to guide your eyes whenever you are reading. If you don't have a pen, use your hand and follow a finger. Even when reading for high comprehension, guiding your way through a text with a physical item or finger will make reading easier and more effective.

Tips on How to Practice These Techniques

It will take time and practice to become proficient at using the previous techniques. In particular, when using a pace maker to force higher reading speeds you may struggle to keep up.

If very poor comprehension continues consistently with any technique, then cut down your work periods. Consider taking five minutes to practice a technique followed by a five minute break. Once you have become comfortable with this, try adding five minutes to the practice time.

Patience and consistent practice is the name of the game here. Don't worry if what you're reading makes no sense and just isn't "going in." It won't at first, and it might not for a while. Reading in these new ways is a significant adjustment for your mind and eyes. This is especially true for the last three techniques:

grouping, eliminating subvocalization, and forcing speed with a pace maker.

It helps to monitor progress in order to build momentum and confidence in your new reading skills. Re-measure your word-per-minute score regularly, and take notes on comprehension and how you felt during reading.

If after thorough practice you find you aren't managing even limited comprehension with one or more of the techniques, then just use those techniques that you are having success with. Perhaps speed reading for you becomes simply moving your eyes less, but you still sub-vocalize and regress. If that happens, it's fine! You are still going faster and can always come back to try and integrate another technique later.

This concludes section one. From here on, I will refer to the previous "direct" speed reading techniques as simply "speed reading techniques". Therefore, apply whatever form of direct speed reading you have developed with these techniques. Together with the non-direct speed reading techniques we are about to cover, your reading speed will dramatically increase.

The next section is on non-direct speed reading techniques. These will give your reading even more speed. We will also address techniques that focus on comprehension and retention. Throughout we will work to integrate these various techniques into multi-step strategies that will allow you to accomplish a variety of reading goals.

Section Two: Non-Direct Speed Reading, Comprehension, Retention, and Becoming an Effective Reader

Introduction to Section Two

This section of the book will present a more developed, complex understanding of what it is to be an effective reader. You will learn techniques that focus on high value areas. These techniques can boost comprehension, retention, and speed. I refer to techniques like these as "non-direct" because when using them, you often skip text rather than "read" it. These techniques are closer to those used when "skimming" or "scanning" a book. In addition, in this section you will learn techniques that focus solely on boosting comprehension and/or retention.

The following techniques can be thought of as modules that complement the skillset you developed in section one. Together, they form multi-step reading strategies. These multi-step strategies can be tailored to meet a variety of reading goals.

With each technique I will explain how to perform it, the benefits of using it, and suggest where within a reading strategy it would best fit. At the end of this section, I will offer a variety of examples of multi-step reading strategies.

Below, again, is a diagram that illustrates the layout of this book and how it relates to an example multi-step reading strategy.

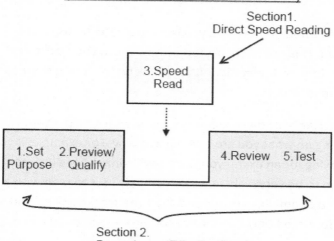

An Example Multi Step Reading Strategy
(and this book's 2 section format)

Section1.
Direct Speed Reading

3.Speed Read

1.Set   2.Preview/
Purpose Qualify

4.Review   5.Test

Section 2.
Becoming an Effective Reader,
non-direct speed reading,
retention and comprehension

Comprehension and Retention

Apart from speed, the other two main objectives when reading are comprehension and retention. Comprehension is synonymous with "understanding" - the degree to which you comprehend a text simply signifies how well you understand it. Consider that at least minimal comprehension is necessary in any kind of reading, as reading without understanding is pointless.

Retention refers to how well you remember the material you have read. This can be measured by how much you remember and how long you remember it for (think deposits into short and long term memory).

The importance of these elements, along with speed, will vary depending on what you are reading and why. For example, if you are studying for an exam, you want both comprehension and retention to be very high, in which case it is best to read with a strategy that amplifies comprehension and retention first and pushes for speed only if it doesn't compromise the initial two.

There are many connections between retention and comprehension in reading. Normally, boosting either one causes the other to be improved as well. Unfortunately, when attempting to boost retention and/or comprehension, speed will often be compromised. However, by intelligently applying reading techniques, all three aspects can be improved compared to normal reading.

Multiple Readings / Phases of Reading for Increased Comprehension, Retention, and Speed

A flawed understanding of reading is the idea that reading once, in a traditional way, is the best way to deal with the majority of texts and reading goals. This is often the only reading philosophy taught in schools. However, it is important to see the value both in reading a text multiple times and in using different reading techniques.

Speed can also be boosted by multiple readings of a text. This allows you to reach the comprehension level you want much faster. For example, it will often be the case that previewing a book (this will be explained soon) and then speed reading it twice will result in improved comprehension and will ultimately be faster than reading a book normally once.

The picture on the next page offers this idea in a simple, comparative bar chart.

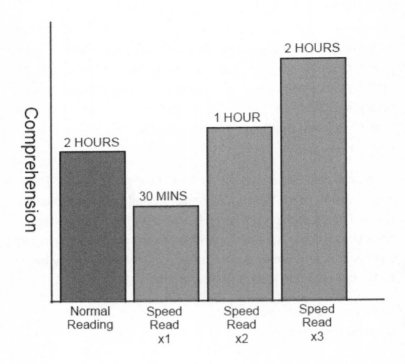

For many people, reading at 600wpm (words per minute) twice, as opposed to reading a text once at 200 wpm, will provide greater comprehension. And because the overall time spent reading a text twice at 600 wpm is still much lower, it's a no-brainer as to which option is best.

The bar chart and wpm comparisons above are hypothetical examples demonstrating the principle of multiple readings. The actual times and comprehension gains for different strategies will vary according to your proficiency at speed reading, the nature of the text, etc.

Setting Your Purpose: Why are you Reading?

In order to become an effective reader, it is important to begin the habit of setting a clear purpose for a book before you begin reading. Setting a purpose will usually be the first stage in any multi-step reading strategy because your purpose will dictate which reading techniques you will utilize.

Your purpose can be applied to two levels. First, you must determine what your overall purpose for reading is. Second, decide what your purpose for reading this specific book is. An example of an overall purpose is: "Research a new career." An example of a book-specific purpose is: "What training do I need to become a lawyer, and what salary can I expect?"

Setting these two purposes won't always be necessary. If you are reading for pleasure, you can take your time with a book without worry. However, on many occasions taking time to set a clear purpose for your overall reading, and/or for the specific book you are reading, will help ensure you read more effectively. Effective reading can be understood as "reading with the right techniques to meet your purpose." When the purpose is implicit, such as enjoying a fiction book, you don't need to set the purpose. But most of the time, a clear purpose will produce more effective reading as you can tailor your reading technique/s accordingly. You can match the purpose with a strategy that gives you the comprehension and retention you need, in the least amount of time.

Qualifying Books

A clear overall purpose also allows you to better filter books and so only read those that give you the information you need. This can help save a great deal of time overall because, obviously, you then only read books that are helpful and avoid the ones that are not.

Often you will not need to qualify a book, but if you are researching/studying/learning it will prove useful. Qualifying a book means ascertaining whether the book will allow you to complete your purpose for reading. It involves discovering whether a book contains what you are looking for, before reading it.

An example of an overall reading purpose is: "Research and find reasons why Napoleon lost the Battle of Waterloo." For this purpose, you can say that a book will be useful if it contains information about the reasons Napoleon lost the Battle of Waterloo. If you pick up a book and can tell it won't fulfill the above criteria, then of course you can put it aside and not read it. This can save you a tremendous amount of time, as you don't waste time reading the wrong books.

Consider also that qualifying a book based on quality is important. Why not try to read the best books you can? Look at reviews and critical opinions from others to do this. Working with technology makes this easier. You can search for critiques online, or simply look at reviews on the Amazon website to reveal the quality of a book.

Previewing: An Essential Preliminary Reading Technique and How to Qualify a Book

The process of "previewing" is the best way to qualify a book and see whether it is worth reading or not. It is also a valuable reading technique in itself and can be considered as another "non-direct" speed reading technique.

Essentially, previewing is a technique that addresses the highest value areas of a book. To preview a book, read the following list slowly, normally, and ideally whilst taking notes. If you are doing this to qualify a book, stop reading/previewing as soon as you realize the book won't be of help to you. Then begin the hunt for another book that might.

To preview, read in order:

Title of the book

The blurb on the back

Contents page

Any details just inside the covers (details that pertain to content, not ISBN, etc.)

Introduction to the book

Conclusion to the book

Introduction to each chapter

Conclusion to each chapter

Smaller secondary headings

Boxed and underlined ideas

Going through the entire list above would be a very thorough and exhaustive preview. Performing the first six would be sufficient for most purposes.

The previewing process alone will sometimes provide enough information to complete your purpose for reading. When only a few ideas or basic comprehension is needed, the limited but strong summarizing nature of previewing is often enough.

SIDE NOTE

I use the phrase "high-value" to mean parts of the text that have the most "top-down" explanations. These are sections that explain the wider ideas, not the details. However, if your purpose is to find specific pieces of information, it is of course going to be these parts of the text that are high-value.

Set a Clear, Book-Specific Purpose

Once you have established that a book qualifies to be read, it is helpful to set a specific purpose for the book. A clear purpose for the book itself allows you to qualify passages of text as you are reading. You can then skip the unimportant parts (those that don't give you what you want). Setting a purpose for your overall reading allows you to skip unhelpful books, and similarly, setting a book-specific purpose enables you to skip unhelpful parts of the text.

The clearer and more specific the goal is, the better. Specific goals will make it easier to ascertain which parts of the text are helpful and which are not as you read. If your goal doesn't lend itself to specificity, it can help to manipulate it so that it is more specific. An example of doing this might be beginning with the book purpose, "find out why Napoleon lost the Battle of Waterloo," and then altering it into something clearer, such as, "find the three most significant reasons that Napoleon lost the Battle of Waterloo". With a more specific goal for reading in place, you can filter through the text and see what is extraneous and what is useful more easily.

Setting a purpose for each chapter is a further extension of this principle. At the start of each chapter, ask yourself the question, "what do I want from this chapter?" or, "what do I want to find in this chapter?" As you are reading, you can then see more clearly what material is extraneous and can be skipped. Upon finishing the chapter, take the time to determine whether or not you found the necessary information.

By integrating the techniques we have learnt so far, we can create an example "multi-step reading strategy" that looks like this:

Set purpose for reading

Qualify by previewing

Set purpose for the book

Speed read, skipping the unimportant

Extended Previewing and Creating an Overview/Summary

The process of previewing a book naturally lends itself to creating an overview of a book. This is also known as creating a summary. The overview/summary might entail a series of points on a page or perhaps a diagram laying out the most important elements of the text. It is simply a unique collection of the most important elements of the book.

Writing out a summary before you begin to properly read a book may seem odd, but doing so will enable you to map out the book and understand it essentially. This clarification of the book's core ideas will prime your conscious and subconscious minds so they know what to expect in the text, and can then better engage with the text in subsequent readings.

The summary can also be a powerful re-introduction to the text if you come back to the book at a later point. If the book is your own and you will be returning to "the shelf" at a later date, you can simply put the summary inside the front cover. If you come back to the book months or years later, looking at the overview will allow you to pick up exactly where you left off before.

Creating a summary can be another technique/module that fits into a multi-step reading strategy. Below is another example of how these modules might come together.

Set purpose for reading

Qualify by previewing

Set purpose for the book

Develop preview into summary

Set purpose for Chapter 1

Speed read Chapter 1

High Value Text is Often at the Start and at the End

You may have noticed that previewing often concentrates on the start and end of sections. This is because it is here that the high-value areas normally are. The introduction and conclusion of any length of writing will have the highest value density, as it is here that the main point and the most important evidence are summarized together.

Typically, text longer than a sentence adheres to the following format:

Introduction: States the main point and central idea.

Body: A series of points that give evidence/explanation/elaboration of the main point.

Conclusion: Re-emphasis of the main point stated in the introduction that is tied together with the ideas developed in the body. A handy mnemonic for remembering this can be 1+2=3. What is stated in the intro, 1, and body, 2, is then brought together in the conclusion, 3. Hence, 1+2=3.

The above format is true for paragraphs, chapters, and the whole book. All will have an introduction, a body, and a conclusion.

To obtain the comprehension you need at the fastest speed, focus on the start and end of each paragraph and chapter. Doing so will mean you read the essential, high value areas of the text first.

To what extent you focus on the start and the end of sections will depend on how much detail you need in order to meet your purpose for reading. Often, just the start and conclusion of a book or chapter will offer enough information. Rarely will your purpose dictate that you need to focus on the body of each paragraph.

To improve your awareness of where the high value areas are in a text, take a pen and underline or highlight these areas. (Remember, focus on the start and end.)

High Value Signposts: Transition Words

As well as taking into account the form of a text (intro, body, conclusion: 1+2=3) to find high value areas, you can also focus on higher value sentences within a text. Being able to pick out and focus on these can further boost your overall speed, comprehension, and retention. These high value phrases are often preceded by "transition" words. Recognizing these words and then slowing down to give more attention to what follows will mean that you read still more effectively.

Examples of transition words:

Consequently

Therefore

Because

Importantly

Furthermore

When you see words such as these, it will usually be a sign that what follows will be of higher value. Taking notes, underlining, or simply slowing down your reading speed may improve your comprehension of these high value ideas (more on these ideas to follow).

Varying Speed

When intelligently applying multiple reading techniques and speed reading, it is best practice to frequently alter your reading speed. Varying the speed at which you read is an excellent way to make sure you give more time to the areas of higher value.

Slower reading, and especially sub-vocalizing each word, will give a small lift to comprehension. This is not just applicable for different texts, but also within the same text. Altering reading speed throughout a book means that you will drop in and out of speed reading modes in order to dovetail with the value/difficulty of each section. Your WPM (words per minute) reading speed will, therefore, fluctuate up and down to align with what you are reading.

Although I am suggesting slowing down for high value areas, I am not suggesting that speed reading doesn't cater for good comprehension; it does. Subvocalization and slow reading simply ensure better comprehension. Similarly, even greater comprehension can be attained if we actually speak aloud when reading. (Do you ever find yourself reading something aloud when you really don't "get it"?)

However, we do not usually need the comprehension that comes with subvocalization, and still rarer do we need to say a word or phrase aloud to understand it.

To clarify, it is practical to speed read and not sub-vocalize most of the time, because the text is usually not sufficiently valuable or difficult. When it does become more valuable and/or difficult, subvocalization or reading aloud provides the needed boost in comprehension.

Read the Majority of Non-Fiction the Same Way You Read a Newspaper

Newspapers are an exceptionally good source for reading quickly. This is because the layout of a newspaper and the way it is written is designed to be as easy as possible to find and read the "high-value" sections.

Newspaper articles are written so that the most important ideas are laid out first. Details are then incrementally added (this is less true for features and opinion pieces). This means that you can read news articles from the start but stop at the point at which you feel you have enough detail. If the first paragraph explains the main point, and that is all you need, you can stop there. Often the first paragraph alone will offer enough information.

If you don't currently practice the previous reading techniques when reading newspapers, e.g., focusing on high value, altering speed, multiple readings, etc. consider beginning here, as newspapers are an easy place to start speed reading. Consider also how it may be helpful to treat the majority of non-fiction as if it were a newspaper. Read only what you want or need to and stop when you obtain enough information.

More Tips for Comprehension and Retention

The following tips will help to boost retention and comprehension levels whilst reading. Use these alongside the previous techniques and principles whenever needed. Specific occasions when retention and comprehension might be especially valuable include studying, test preparation, revising, difficult reading, and technical reading.

Technique 1 - Measure retention and comprehension by asking yourself questions about the text after you have read it.

In order to measure how well you have understood a piece of writing, as well as how effectively you have retained it, answer questions regarding the text once you have finished. Ideally, these questions are specific to the text, but it can be just as helpful (and a lot easier) to try to recall the most important key points.

How many points you try to recall will depend on the information density of the text and what level of comprehension/retention you need. The higher the comprehension/retention you need, the more key points you should try to recall. For example, if you are studying a textbook, perhaps attempt to write down five key points every 500 words.

Reading whilst aware that you need to recall key points later will itself increase comprehension/retention since it will bring more focus and urgency to your reading.

<u>Technique 2 - Put marks at the end of each page to monitor comprehension.</u>

If comprehension is important, and you don't want to go through a text without understanding everything in it, it is helpful to make a note of your comprehension as you go. To do this, after reading a page put a little cross at the bottom if you felt your comprehension wasn't good enough or a tick if it was. You can then return to the pages marked with "X's" later and re-read them.

(This is only possible if the material doesn't build on itself, i.e. you don't need to understand page one to understand page two.)

This is also an excellent way to gauge whether your average reading speed should be increased or decreased. Consider that if you are placing more crosses than ticks at the bottom of the pages, your comprehension isn't good enough, and you may need to slow your reading down. If you rarely put any crosses, perhaps on one in eight pages or less, speed up.

(Ignore this technique when first learning to "direct" speed read with the techniques you learnt in section one. You will have to persevere through bad comprehension until your mind adjusts to direct speed reading.)

Technique 3 - Repeat exposure and "cram" material for short term recall.

In order to effectively retain information into your short term memory (NOT long term), re-read and repeatedly expose yourself to the material.

Technique 4 - For still better memorization (and long term recall), practice active recall.

Reviewing and attempting to actively recall (remember from memory) is an even better way to retain information. This is especially the case for long term memorization. Actively recall material regularly in order to deposit it into your long term memory.

Technique 5 - Teach and/or discuss material to both comprehend and retain.

To improve your comprehension and retention of a text, discuss and attempt to explain what you have read to someone else. Explaining the material to someone else will develop your understanding as you have to re-form the material. It will also re-affirm the memory. Finally, attempting to explain the material well enough for someone else to make sense of it will make you very conscious of whether or not you fully understand it.

Technique 6 - Read critically and imagine discussing and/or debating with the author as you read.

The more you can engage with the material, the more you will understand it. Reading critically will help. To read critically, think about what you agree and disagree with as you read. Imagine debating with the author, and don't accept everything you read at "face value." Perhaps write your criticisms/opinions/ideas in the margin or on another piece of paper. This will help to consolidate and crystalize your thoughts.

Integrating one or more of the above techniques to your reading strategy is a fantastic way to boost comprehension / retention whenever they are needed.

Active Reading: Note Taking as you Read

Whether reading slowly or at speed, adding notes to what you are reading and reading "actively" is a great way to boost comprehension and retention.

Note taking includes:

Underlining and/or highlighting important parts.

Writing down key points in the margin or on another piece of paper.

Writing questions, comments, and opinions in the margin or separate piece of paper.

Drawing diagrams to bring together what you have learnt. These might include mind maps, Venn diagrams, or concept maps.

The greater your interaction with the text, i.e., the more note taking and annotating you do, the higher your comprehension and retention will become.

As always, focus on the more valuable areas of the text, and vary the level of notes and interaction to match your goals. For high comprehension, take a lot of notes. If you are speed reading and only need minimal comprehension, then keep notes light and focus on the most valuable sections of the text.

The Effective Reading Model: Integrating Parts to Form a Strategy

The various techniques and principles we have covered are best utilized by integration into multi-step strategies. These can be personally tailored to fulfill your overall reading purpose.

Below are example strategies for a series of different reading purposes. This list is not exhaustive, nor definitive. Mix and match steps to create the best strategies for you and your reading.

(Each strategy follows on from first establishing your overall reading purpose.)

Purpose: Search for simple information. (Stop as soon as info is found.)

Clarify what you want to find. Deconstruct it, and set a book-specific purpose

Preview

Extended preview, create summary

Speed read

Repeat step 4 until you find information you want

Purpose: Search for more detailed, specific information. (Stop as soon as info is found.)

Clarify what you want to find. Deconstruct it, and set a book-specific purpose

Preview

Extended preview, create summary

Speed read

Slow read until you find information you want

Purpose: To understand the text basically. (Minimal comprehension.)

Preview

Extended preview, create summary

Speed read

Purpose: Good Comprehension

Preview

Extended preview, create summary

Speed read

Speed read with note taking

Repeat step 4

Purpose: Great Comprehension

Preview

Extended preview, create summary

Speed read

Speed read with note taking

Slow read

Purpose: High Retention. (Perhaps for a test.)

Create questions and/or goals for what material you want to retain

Preview

Extended preview, create summary

Clarify/alter what you wrote for step 1 if you have reason to

Speed read

Speed read with note taking

Create test questions

"Cram" if test is soon; actively recall answers if test is at a later date

Purpose: Reading Critically

Preview

Extended preview, create summary

Create questions to answer

Speed read with notes

Slow read with notes

Return to questions

SQ3R and PQRST

I will now present two pre-existing reading strategies used by many readers. They are proven methods that target comprehension and retention. Both, especially SQ3R, are foundational for many students. Much of the previous work in this book is owed to their success.

SQ3R

Introduced by Francis Ford Pleasant Robinson in his 1946 book *Effective Study[j]*.

Survey: Gain a basic understanding of the text. This is "previewing" as we have learnt it.

Question: Write down questions you want answered through reading the book (similar to establishing a book-specific purpose.)

Read: Read through the text (normally, slowly) and attempt to answer the questions. Write bullet points, highlight, and take notes.

Recite: Write up the answers you found to the questions asked in step 2.

Review: Go over the text again. Look over notes and your answers.

PQRST[ii]

Preview: Preview the text through summaries, introductions, and conclusions.

Question: Write questions about the text that you want to answer through reading.

Read: Read the text at normal pace.

Summary: Create a summary (synonymous with overview) of the text. Write down the most important points in notes and diagrams - everything that you have learnt.

Test: Return to the questions you asked in step 2 and attempt to answer them.

Read Multiple Books on a Topic and Learn from Multiple Forms of Information (Syntopic Learning)

An excellent technique to increase comprehension and speed is to read multiple texts on a topic. It can also help to learn from multiple forms, e.g., audio, reading, conversation, and video. By reading and/or learning from different forms, it is easy to gain multiple perspectives, thereby developing improved comprehension. This will also ensure that you gain complete coverage of a topic. Reading multiple texts to develop comprehension was first proposed by Mortimor J. Adler in his book *How to Read.* He called this "syntopic reading."[iii]

Comprehension can be developed excellently when the mind is exposed to an idea in a multitude of ways. When reading a series of books on a given topic, we learn about the same things but with different explanations, different examples, and subtly different takes on the topic. Thanks to these different perspectives, we can develop a more complete understanding.

Not only does a variety of explanations of the same information help our understanding, so too does interacting with information in different forms. By learning from different forms, e.g., text, audio, conversation, video etc. we create different forms of memory including visual, emotional, and audio. This strengthens comprehension as you experience the topic in a multitude of ways. Learning through a variety of mediums also makes it more likely that you will engage your preferred learning style(s), and consequently, play to your strengths and learn more effectively.

Another benefit of reading multiple books and using numerous forms of information is that you can ensure (or at least increase the likelihood) that all the material you need is covered. On the next page there are two pictures that express this:

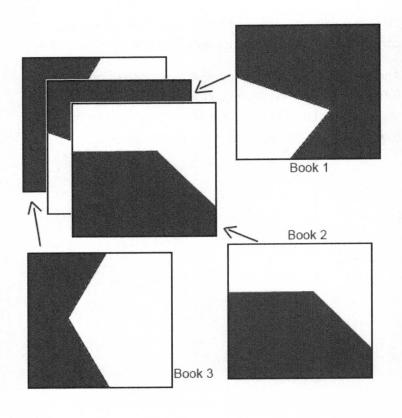

Book 1

Book 2

Book 3

Whereby...

Total Coverage of Required Material	No Coverage of Required Material
	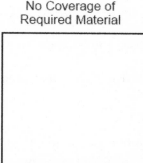

Use syntopic reading and/or learning to develop understanding through multiple perspectives and to ensure you cover all the material you need.

Creating the Right Environment and Conditions for Reading

There are various things you can do to improve the effectiveness of your reading before you even open a book. The following are the building blocks of creating good reading conditions:

Good lighting. You never want to be straining your eyes. Get a lamp.

Make sure you are wearing glasses if you need them. This is perhaps obvious but needs to be said.

Read in a relaxed but alert state: breathe, stretch, or take a walk if needed.

Practice good posture with a straight back and relaxed shoulders.

Sit back in a chair that supports your neck and shoulders.

In addition, experiment with your reading environment to boost your focus and enjoyment whilst reading. If you haven't already, consider the following, and see what works well for you.

Sound:

Music: classical, rock, high tempo, low tempo

Silence (ear plugs)

White noise

Location:

Park bench

In nature: woods, fields, a beach

Alone in a room

Café/Bar

Candles/Incense

Moving images in background:

TV/Film playing in the background (muted)

Other People: Café/Bar

Which environment works best will often depend on what you are reading and why. If you are studying complex material, reading alone in a quiet, well-lit room will often be preferred. However, for casual reading for pleasure, sitting on the beach listening to your favorite band might work. It won't always be obvious what works best. For example, fast paced rock music can help some people to concentrate. If you haven't already, think about experimenting with these aspects in order to enjoy and get more from your reading.

Practicing and Enjoying Reading and Becoming a "Book-Worm"

The techniques we have explored will require varying amounts of time to master. The "direct" speed reading techniques in section one necessitate time set aside regularly and will alter how you interact with text at a more fundamental level. Learning to group words and eliminate sub-vocalization in particular will involve working through phases of poor comprehension and frustration.

The material in section two and building multi-step reading strategies will be easier to learn. However, whatever the technique, there will always be the need to practice. Also, make sure to push yourself to learn techniques that seem alien. The techniques that seem the trickiest and make the least sense may well be the ones that end up offering the most improvement to your reading.

BONUS SECTION: HOW TO STUDY

Introduction

The aim of this book is to give you tips to make your time studying as successful and enjoyable as possible. It contains my best advice on time management, goal setting, and how to get the best grades with the least effort. It's advice that also transfers brilliantly well to professionals, the self-employed, and anyone who manages their own projects and/or daily work cycle.

(If you fall into the non-student category, whenever you see the word "study" throughout this book, think the word "work" instead, and whenever you see "grades" think "work goals".)

There's nothing more to say, so let's get started!

Build the Study Habit and Schedule Study Times

One of the main reasons students don't get good grades is simple: they don't have the study habit. Being able to regularly make yourself sit down and learn the necessary material is an essential part of becoming a great student.

Both when you study and the length of time you study for should be as regular and routine as possible. This will make the habit of studying easier to begin and sustain over time. Working at the same time every day is the best way to do this, e.g., between 7 and 9 every morning. (This time works well as it is before classes.) Of course, your study time will depend on the courses you are taking and your other commitments.

Working at set times every day will help build the habit of studying. There will be less urge to procrastinate and do unimportant tasks because you know when you should be working and when you shouldn't. Eventually it will actually take more willpower not to study at these times because you will subconsciously expect to be utilizing your study time.

Time Box Tasks

To build a sense of urgency and avoid being overwhelmed with work, it is helpful to create definite periods of time or 'time boxes' in which you work.

Set a timer and do not work for more or less than the time you set. Then, take a break for a small timed period. Rinse and repeat. Working like this will help you overcome procrastination because you will not feel the sense of being overwhelmed by a project. One of the main reasons that students (or anyone) procrastinate is that they feel anxious about not knowing how to begin and/or that they will have to keep working for a long time. By limiting the time spent working on something to a set number, we can alleviate anxiety caused by either of these problems.

Working for a definite amount of time also helps stop perfectionism and curbs the desire to spend more time on a project than is necessary. Many people suffer from this. They work long hours to make their project as perfect as it can possibly be. Sometimes this leads to people doing great things. However, it is more often an enemy of productivity as it leads to a task dragging on for longer than needed. For example, if it takes 10 hours to complete an assignment to a 70 percent standard, is it worth working 20 hours to complete it to a 72 percent standard? Sometimes yes, but usually no. Time boxing is an excellent tool for stopping perfectionism in its tracks. It forces us to complete a task to a good standard and no more.

Both for study sessions and for whole projects, many students find they work more effectively by working to a time scale. In doing so, you will create a greater sense of urgency to your work, as you only think about continuing work until the timer sounds. The alternative of working for an unspecified amount of time makes both beginning and continuing work more difficult. It also encourages a slow, non-urgent work mode and/or perfectionism. To avoid this, use time boxing and set time limits for your work.

Prioritize Assignments and Be Aware of Grade Boundaries/Percentages

The extent to which a project affects your grade and how long it takes to complete will vary in relation to one another. Therefore, it is important to spend more time on those projects that contribute more marks and less on those that don't.

At the beginning of the academic year, you should deconstruct your course so that you know what percentage each module/exam/project will contribute toward the final grade. This will reveal which areas require more time and effort than others. It will often not be clear what the more valuable modules are until you do this.

You can then place more emphasis on the areas that contribute more to your overall grade and limit time spent on the less valuable. Re-adjust where you are placing your time and effort as you receive feedback throughout the year. Be flexible and note where you are struggling to get the grades you want. When you receive marks for coursework, rework these into your plans. For example, if you do very well in a piece of coursework, scale back the time you planned to spend revising for its corresponding exam, and instead, prepare for an exam on a topic you are struggling with. There is no way to perfectly balance this, as it will be based on guesswork. Simply do your best, and work as intelligently as you can.

Test Yourself Frequently

Always being aware of exactly how well you are progressing toward your final grade is essential in order to adjust your study plans and better understand what you need to work on. Apart from coursework and feedback in class, testing yourself is the best way to do this.

Gather past exam papers/questions and frequently test yourself with them. Ideally, use entire test papers from previous years (assuming the course hasn't changed too drastically). Also, test yourself in conditions similar to how you will take the actual exam. Giving yourself the same amount of time as you will get in the real exam is crucial. Set a timer and stick to it. Once you have completed the exam paper, mark it yourself or give it to a teacher/lecturer/fellow student to mark. Make sure whoever is marking it does so by following a correct answer sheet/mark scheme.

Ascertaining what level you are currently working at will reveal where your subsequent studies should concentrate. For example, if you are working on an essay-based exam, you might learn that the content of your writing is fine, but the quantity needs to increase. In this case, you can take further practice tests and simply work to write faster.

Start Work Early

Many people find studying in the morning works best for them. Try this yourself and see if you can join the club. Getting your studies out of the way first thing is an excellent way to get more studying done.

Starting work early is often easier because there is less chance of getting distracted and becoming involved doing other things. Watching TV, Internet browsing, or relaxing with friends are often best left until after you have done your studying. These activities then become rewards instead of distractions, and you can enjoy the rest of the day without worry that you should have done more. Studying earlier in the day within a definite "time box," before you have a chance to get distracted by anything else, is a great way to increase the efficiency of your studying and enjoy your days more.

Have Fun Away From Your Studies

If you work intelligently, there is no need to work non-stop. Plan many breaks, and arrange for fun! Enjoyable activities boost your focus and memory. In the same way that muscles need rest after exercise to grow, so too your mind needs to relax after it is exerted.

It is helpful to get as far away as possible from your study and work habits. Take time to travel to another city, another country, or simply try to do something new. Getting away and having fun will mean that when you do return to studying, you will be completely ready to learn, to work hard, and get the best grades you are capable of.

Create Study Routines: 60-60-30, 50-50-10

Creating definite study routines will allow you to better manage your time. It is difficult and unsustainable to work constantly for hours at a time, so implement regular patterns in which you alternate between working and taking breaks. This is short-scale time boxing applied to a rigorous work/rest pattern.

Experiment with what works best for you as different stretches of concentration work well for different people. Some prefer a longer four hour work session to get into "flow," while others prefer shorter ones so as to never feel overwhelmed by a project.

An example work/rest study routine that fits well into a normal day is to work for a 50 minute period followed by a 10 minute break, and every four hours take an hour break for a meal.

However, there are no hard and fast rules. You might prefer to work for 90 minutes at a time, and then take a 30 minute break. The aim is to find what works well for you so that you can sustain working for a long period of time with good focus and minimum fatigue.

If you feel exhausted or too mentally strained with a routine, then work for smaller cycles. You can always increase the work time lengths if it seems doable later.

Make sure to always use a timer, and stop working when it sounds, even if you want to continue. You often won't be aware that you need a break when you actually do. If you become successful with this habit, you will find you can create work-rest routines that are generative and allow you to work with focus for 6, 8, 10, or even 12 hour days whilst still feeling good.

Minimize Possible Distractions and Eliminate Multi-Tasking

One of the greatest enemies to successful work in the modern age is the abundance of distractions. When you are studying, it is imperative to make sure that you study and do nothing else. Your ability to focus all of your attention on the task at hand is a powerful asset. Attempting to do more than one thing at a time or switching between activities jeopardizes this.

Turn off your mobile phone and close the internet browser. If these remain a possible distraction, make it as difficult as possible to access them. For example, turn off your phone and put it out of sight or out of reach. Consider giving it to a friend or leaving it in another room until you are finished working.

These distractions will compromise how effectively you work, and even worse, can lead to you stopping work altogether. Just checking a website or your phone for a moment can cause a series of internal triggers, and in no time you will lose the motivation and focus you had. This can be a big obstacle for students and employees alike. If this sounds like your past studying attempts, make eliminating distractions a priority.

Set Goals for Grades

Setting goals for the grades you want will make it easier to ascertain the level of work required to receive them. The goal of simply "getting the best grades you can" is good, but not good enough. These goals need to be more specific and ideally very specific. Many students already have goals for the grades they want to achieve. If you don't have any, start thinking about what yours could be now.

Having clear goals for the grades you want will make it easier to ascertain what you need to learn in order to achieve them. This is partly achieved by saving you from wasting time learning things you don't need to. Some skills and information might take a lot of time to learn, but if they are beyond what you need to learn it will be a waste of time. For example, for an essay-based exam, there is no use learning a large amount of quotations (enough to get an A) if your target is a B grade and your grasp of concepts isn't nearly strong enough to get a B.

Goals for grades will also allow you to celebrate successes and push you to do more when needed.

Once you have decided what your target grades are, find out precisely what you need to work on in order to achieve them. Then build your study schedule around working on these areas (with regular testing to ensure you are progressing well).

Clarify Study Session Goals

Every time you sit down to study, you should be clear about what you are going to do and what you want to gain from the session. Planning to "study for module A" won't be nearly as effective as "50 minutes reading and annotating chapter 1." It is far too easy to study aimlessly while naively believing that you are learning. Working in this fuzzy, diffused way will often mean you don't learn or progress in your work. Instead, have focused, clear targets each time you sit.

At the end of the study session, you will also be able to check off the task, and this will also help you feel more motivated to continue on. The sense of incremental progress with each completed study session will build momentum and make each successive study session easier.

Detach from Work While on Breaks

When you take a short break from work, it is very important that you really do take a break.

If you are studying at a computer screen (perhaps you are writing up some lecture notes), the break you take must be away from the computer. If you are taking only 10 minute breaks every hour, it is important to make this break a time for your mind and body to separate from what you have been working on.

If you are working at a computer, opening a new browser and checking a news channel or a social networking site is no longer working, but is it truly taking a break? Not really. Instead, move away from the desk and away from the computer. Do something physical. Maybe take a walk or lie down. At the very least, don't look at a screen. The break needs to be spent on something different from what you have been doing. If you have been sitting at a computer screen, lying down outside on the grass for 10 minutes could help you to unwind sufficiently.

You might find it helpful to engage your mind with something else altogether. If you don't engage your mind with something else, like a video game or book, you might find your mind racing on with what you were doing. To get more mental separation and a better break, consider doing something that takes your attention away from what you were working on altogether.

Why are you at School/College/University?

Knowing exactly what you want from your course and what you are going to do afterward will further help you to focus and study well.

Perhaps you are career-driven and want to go into a certain industry after your course. If this is the case, research the job role you want, how much money you want to be earning, where you want to work, etc. Getting details will help you feel grounded and motivated to continue on with the course.

For some students, there is no definite job role at the end. This does not mean that you cannot find a clear purpose for studying hard. Maybe you enjoy the subject and want to study it for this reason alone. If this is the case, consider concrete things you can do to get more from it. This could be getting an article in your field published.

Understanding why you are studying and what you really want from your course is a great way to further boost your focus and enjoyment.

Find a Study Partner and/or a Study Group

Studying with other people is a great way to get more from your course.

Depending on your preferences for working and your personality, this can be a fantastic prospect or a daunting one. However, creating a study group, or at the very least one person with whom you regularly work, can help a lot. Explaining topics and quizzing one another will boost your comprehension and ensure that you thoroughly understand the material.

Make sure you choose the right people to study with. It might not be best to study with a friend you also go out partying with. Additionally, make sure you study with people of a similar ability. 'Carrying' someone who is struggling won't be productive.

Working in a group can be a brilliant idea as well. This can be the most enjoyable way to work, especially if you are naturally highly social. Working in a group helps you to motivate one another and can provide many points of view.

Perfect Necessary Skills and Seek Feedback

There will inevitably be skills within your subject you need to master. These skills will usually require someone else to critique your ability. Seek as much feedback as possible in order to improve these skills.

Whether you are working in a laboratory or writing essays, the skills you have to develop cannot be marked and improved on entirely by yourself. You need an expert. This person will often be a teacher assigned to you. It might then be a matter of luck how helpful their critiques are and whether they are offered as regularly as you require them. If they aren't offered enough or aren't helpful enough, seek another tutor from the establishment to replace and/or work alongside to provide extra help.

In cases such as essay writing, you will need to practice regularly. Practice even if your work won't be marked. The more feedback you can get the better, so it doesn't hurt to ask other teachers to critique your work as well.

Whatever the skill set you are trying to develop, practice properly, practice regularly, seek feedback and then improve. Use this process again and again, until you develop your skill set into an art form.

Build a Relationship with a Tutor/Mentor

Having a go-between for you and your school/establishment will prove very helpful. Many centers will provide you with a 'tutor,' i.e., someone you meet with regularly in order to discuss your progress. If yours doesn't provide this extra help, find someone who can take on this role for you.

Your tutor can provide guidance for your course and let you know what to expect. He or she can answer questions on any number of things. For example, a tutor might help you to find old exam papers to work from, or find out where an exam will be seated.

If anything goes wrong during your course and you need help (perhaps you fall ill and need an extension on a project), help and advice from your tutor could be essential. Also, if you have moved away from home and need guidance on everyday issues, for example, money management, eating out, etc. Having someone older who can guide you will make life easier.

Thank you

Thank you for making it to the end of both books. If you enjoyed them, please leave a review on the Amazon website.

All the best,

John Connelly

---

[i] Robinson, Francis Pleasant (1978). *Effective Study* (6th ed.). New York: Harper & Row.

[ii] Gopalakrishnan, Karthika (2009-01-08). "Students tackle stress as board exams draw". *The Times Of India*.

[iii] Mortimer Adler, *How to Read a Book: The Art of Getting a Liberal Education*, (1940)

Made in the USA
Las Vegas, NV
05 May 2024

89549786R00042